At the Top of Their Game

Serena Williams

Setting New Standards

Gerry Boehme

Cavendish Square
New York

Published in 2018 by Cavendish Square Publishing, LLC
243 5th Avenue, Suite 136, New York, NY 10016

Copyright © 2018 by Cavendish Square Publishing, LLC
First Edition

This publication represents the opinions and views of the author based on his or her personal experience, knowledge, and research. The information in this book serves as a general guide only. The author and publisher have used their best efforts in preparing this book and disclaim liability rising directly or indirectly from the use and application of this book.

CPSIA Compliance Information: Batch #CS17CSQ

All websites were available and accurate when this book was sent to press.
Library of Congress Cataloging-in-Publication Data

Names: Boehme, Gerry, author.
Title: Serena Williams : Setting New Standards / Gerry Boehme.
Description: New York : Cavendish Square Publishing, 2018. | Series: At the Top of Their Game | Includes bibliographical references and index.
Identifiers: LCCN 2016050896 (print) | LCCN 2016059257 (ebook) | ISBN 9781502627629 (library bound) | ISBN 9781502627636 (E-book)
Subjects: LCSH: Williams, Serena, 1981---Juvenile literature. | African American women tennis players--Biography--Juvenile literature. | Women tennis players--United States--Biography--Juvenile literature.
Classification: LCC GV994.W55 B64 2018 (print) | LCC GV994.W55 (ebook) | DDC 796.342092 [B] --dc23
LC record available at "https://lccn.loc.gov/2016050896" https://lccn.loc.gov/2016050896

Editorial Director: David McNamara
Editor: Fletcher Doyle
Copy Editor: Rebecca Rohan
Associate Art Director: Amy Greenan
Designer: Jessica Nevins
Production Coordinator: Karol Szymczuk
Photo Research: J8 Media

Printed in the United States of America

At the Top of Their Game

Contents

Changing the Face of Tennis

Serena Williams is, simply put, a tennis **icon**. During the course of her remarkable career, through the 2017 Australian Open, Serena has won an **open-era** record twenty-three major **tournaments** in **singles**, including the four **Grand Slam** titles at least three times each, as well as an Olympic singles gold medal. In addition, Serena has teamed with her sister Venus to win fourteen Grand Slam **doubles** championships and three Olympic gold medals. Serena has also won two Grand Slams in mixed doubles.

When you look more deeply into Serena's life and career, it becomes clear that she has broken the mold of the typical tennis success story. In fact, Serena has taken that mold and shattered it, piece by piece, until it is almost unrecognizable.

Most tennis players are white; Serena is African American. Most players come from higher-income households; the Williams family lived in a poor, crime-ridden neighborhood outside of Los Angeles. Most players receive expert instruction and join the tennis tour at an early age. Serena was trained by her father after he taught himself

Opposite: Serena Williams displays her 2016 Wimbledon trophy, which was her twenty-second Grand Slam tennis championship.

Known for her fashions beyond tennis, Serena Williams shows off her latest designs during New York Fashion Week in September 2016.

to play; her father also limited Serena's tournament appearances and made sure she pursued other interests.

Few high-ranking players have brothers or sisters who also play tennis at their level. Serena's sister, Venus, stands out as a tennis star in her own right and probably ranks as the toughest opponent Serena has ever faced. Also, most top players excel for only a few short years before they are eclipsed by younger, stronger rivals. Even at the age of thirty-five, twenty years after joining the **professional** tennis tour, Serena continued to dominate tennis.

The Serena Williams story extends far beyond tennis, however. She ranks as one of the highest-paid female athletes in the world. Her fashion designs have attracted attention on the tennis court and graced the covers of magazines including *Glamour* and *Vogue*. Serena has written books and appeared on numerous television programs, including her own reality show. She has been linked romantically to rappers (Drake, Common), athletes (Amar'e Stoudemire, Keyshawn Johnson), actors, directors, and even her coach before announcing her engagement to Reddit cofounder Alexis Ohanian in late 2016.

Serena also gives back. She's built a school in Africa and established a charitable foundation to support education for those in need. In recognition of her work on and off the court, Serena has won many honors and awards, almost too many to count. *Time* magazine has included her on its list of the one hundred most influential people in the world—twice!

In a movie she made about Serena and her sister Venus, director Maiken Baird said, "The story of the Williams sisters is the ultimate American story ... two African American sisters who come from the **ghetto** ... They become number one and number two in the world."

In 2006, Serena told *Tennis* magazine, "They'll always remember Venus and me for starting a whole new **legacy** in tennis and a whole new style. The physical fitness, the running, the **serve**, the return, the fashion. We changed the whole game."

Serena Williams has changed the face of tennis itself.

Chapter 1

The Seeds of Stardom

Serena Williams was raised in the city of Compton, located in south central Los Angeles. Compton was, and still is, a rough area, haunted by poverty, drugs, and gangs. In 2005, a national study ranked all US cities based on crime; Compton finished fourth in the country.

Serena's father, Richard, grew up poor in a primarily African American neighborhood in Shreveport, Louisiana. Richard's mother picked cotton for a living, and she raised him with four sisters after his father abandoned the family. Richard experienced the full effects of racism while growing up in the 1940s and 1950s, a time when the Southern states were **segregated**. He was called terrible names, had to ride in the back of buses, could not eat in certain restaurants, and had to use public facilities reserved for blacks only. Richard's mother taught him to believe in himself despite these difficult experiences.

In his book *Black and White: The Way I See It*, Richard Williams wrote, "It took a long time to understand what [my mother] was trying to teach me—that every person had the responsibility to

Opposite: Serena Williams (*left*) learned to play facing older sister Venus (*right*) on the public courts in poor Compton, California.

make something of himself no matter how people saw him. What you find in life, you deal with."

In the 1970s, Richard moved to Los Angeles. There he met and fell in love with Oracene Price, a nurse with three daughters from a previous relationship. Richard and Oracene married and, shortly after daughter Venus was born in 1980, the family moved to Oracene's hometown of Saginaw, Michigan. Serena Williams was born there in 1981.

In April 1983, the family moved to Compton because, Richard said, he wanted his daughters to grow up in a difficult environment to help them prepare for the hardships they would face in life. He hoped it would help them appreciate what they would later accomplish for themselves.

Oracene had her doubts. She once described Compton as "a suburban ghetto." During the 1980s, gangs ruled the neighborhood, and even the police avoided some areas. She decided to support her husband, however, and agreed to the move.

Serena was now the youngest of five girls in the house. The three oldest—Yetunde, Isha, and Lyndrea—were actually half-sisters to Venus and Serena, but the five thought of themselves as one family and were very close. They all slept in the same bedroom, which had only four beds. Being the youngest, Serena took turns sleeping with each of the other sisters. Serena loved all of her sisters but, being so close in age, she idolized Venus.

After moving to Compton, Richard ran his own security company and a phone-book delivery service, and he also sold affordable health insurance to low-income people in his area. Oracene worked as a nurse. Both parents had big dreams while they were young, and they wanted to pass that quality on to their children.

Richard Williams decided to teach Venus and Serena how to play tennis after watching a women's match on television.

In the early 1900s, women's tennis was considered to be more a social activity than a sport. French champion Suzanne Lenglen, second from left, was a fashion-setter when this photo taken at London's Roehampton Club in 1926.

Tennis Beckons

Neither of Serena's parents had any experience in tennis when they moved to Compton. In fact, relatively few African Americans even played tennis at that time.

The first ladies lawn tennis championship was held in 1884 at Wimbledon, England. The first women's championship was held in the United States three years later. For many years afterwards, tennis was thought to be more of an upper-class social event than a sport for all to play. At first, African Americans played in tournaments along with whites, but they were later banned along racial lines in the early 1900s. African Americans founded a tennis organization of their own in 1916.

The tennis color line was finally broken when Althea Gibson became the first African American to compete in the US National Championship at Forest Hills in 1950. Gibson, an eleven-time Grand Slam champion and now known as the "Jackie Robinson of tennis," was inducted into the Tennis Hall of Fame in 1971.

There have been other African American players since that time. Zina Garrison-Jackson reached the finals at Wimbledon in 1990 and won an Olympic gold medal in 1998. Arthur Ashe became the first African American man to win Wimbledon in 1975. Ashe also won the US Open (1968) and the Australian Open (1970) and later became a famous author, role model, and social activist. Today, the main stadium at the US Open bears his name.

One day, before Venus was born, Richard was watching television, tuned in to the end of a women's tennis match. He watched as Virginia Ruzici won the tournament and received its top prize of $40,000. The amount shocked Richard; Ruzici earned more in one week than he made in an entire year! Richard remembered thinking that Ruzici did not seem like a great athlete. He just assumed she practiced constantly and focused on her sport. He decided right then that he would train his daughters to be tennis stars.

Dad Becomes Coach

Richard Williams had never played tennis, so he had to teach himself before he could teach his daughters. He collected all the tennis books and videotapes he could. He also made his way to the local public courts and insisted that he be allowed to play with the more experienced players who were there. After he learned the game, he taught Oracene to play, and then he introduced tennis to his girls.

Yetunde showed some skill, but she lacked real interest and later decided to pursue a medical career. Isha also had no passion for tennis; she later attended law school. Lyndrea preferred music to sports. Venus and Serena immediately took to the game, however, even at an early age.

Richard gave Venus her first racket when she was four years old and taught her to play on the public tennis courts in the area. That approach stood in stark contrast to what most future tennis stars experienced. They were usually white and were given expensive private lessons with personal tutors at tennis **academies** and country clubs. Venus loved tennis, but she also valued the time alone with her father.

Serena learned about tennis while watching Venus and her father play, and she desperately wanted to join them. She finally did, but she is not sure exactly when. In her autobiography *Serena Williams: On The Line*, Serena wrote that she does not really have a first tennis memory: "I just remember playing, all the time. It's like tennis was always there … Like breathing."

Soon, Serena and Venus were hitting the ball back and forth between them. It was fun but also competitive. "It was like a nuclear war," Serena remembered.

The public tennis courts where Serena and Venus learned to play were old and run-down, with the cement surface cracked and covered with broken glass. Serena and Venus often had to clear garbage off the court in order to practice. Serena's father would invent creative drills and games for the girls in order to make tennis fun. He also would write messages on signs that he would hang around the courts to motivate them to believe in themselves and to plan for success.

The area around the courts could be dangerous as well. According to one story, Richard made a deal with local gang members so that, instead of fighting among themselves, they would guard the courts while the sisters practiced.

A Well-Rounded Life

Serena and Venus were both great athletes and excelled in many sports when they were young, not just tennis. They ran track, played soccer and softball, and participated in gymnastics. Richard and Oracene also stressed the importance of education, and both Serena and Venus were good students. In fact, unless they brought home A's and B's from school, they were not allowed to play tennis until their grades improved.

The Williams family was also very religious. Serena said her parents told their daughters, "Always put God first, even ahead of family." As **Jehovah's Witnesses**, Venus and Serena accompanied their mother as she traveled door-to-door in the neighborhood, giving out reading materials and discussing Bible lessons. Oracene once said that, at first, people could be shocked when she appeared with Venus and Serena at their house and knocked on the door. "They want to talk about tennis, but we want to talk about the Bible."

Choosing Tennis

When she was ten, her parents asked Venus to choose her main sport so she could concentrate and get better. She picked tennis and began to dominate other players. Copying her sister, Serena also chose tennis.

Serena later remembered, "What *didn't* I do to try and copy Venus when I was younger. I mean, her favorite color was my favorite color. Her favorite animal was my favorite animal. She wanted to win Wimbledon. I wanted to win Wimbledon."

While Serena was certainly talented at tennis, she also owned a big advantage over other players her age. Serena practiced mainly against Venus, who was older, stronger, and more advanced and experienced in her game. Her practices were harder than most matches. Like her sister, Serena won most of her local matches in convincing fashion.

Gaining Notice

Both sisters began to attract attention as they played and beat everyone they faced. The story of these two African American sisters, trained by their father on public courts in the ghetto, was almost like a fairy tale. Even before Venus became a teenager, sports agents and marketing representatives from big companies quickly began to approach Richard and Oracene, offering money, cars, and gifts for the chance to sell the Serena and Venus story to the world. It was tempting, but Richard wanted to shield his daughters from too much attention, and he rejected all the offers. He had no doubt that his daughters would become rich and famous, but there would be plenty of time for that.

The United States Tennis Association (USTA) also noticed how well Serena and Venus were playing. The USTA felt that both sisters would need better coaching and competition to get to the next level and pressed Richard to enroll them in the Southern California program.

Richard agreed to let them enter a few USTA age-group tournaments before pulling them off the circuit. He refused to let his daughters be coached by others. He thought Serena and Venus were already doing well under his watch, and that they would learn more by practicing against each other than by competing against other players their age who were not as good.

Smart or Selfish?

Some people at that time believed that Richard was turning into what is known as a bad "tennis parent," someone who is more concerned with their own ego and success than the best interests of their children. Unfortunately, parents like that were not uncommon in tennis, and still aren't, even in the professional ranks. Richard Williams could be loud and bombastic in public and often boasted about how his daughters would become stars. Based on what people saw, it was easy for some to conclude that Richard was one of those "tennis fathers" they had seen so often before.

Oracene, Serena's mother, has been described as the opposite of Richard—soft-spoken and dignified. Together, Richard and Oracene provided balance in the girls' lives. Serena describes Oracene as fun and easygoing. "My father's the arms and legs of the family, but my mother is the spine," Serena once told a group of young girls during a visit to a Harlem school. "Imagine a body without a spine. It would be just a blob."

Richard truly believed that his daughters would revolutionize women's tennis. He and Oracene wanted to shield their girls from the pressures of tennis stardom, at least at so young an age. They protected private family time. They limited the number of tournaments that Serena and Venus could enter. Sometimes, they made the girls stop playing tennis for a while so they would not burn out too early.

By stressing balance in their lives, Serena's parents helped instill the idea that tennis was only one part of a greater whole, and that she and Venus also had to prepare for their lives after tennis ended. Oracene and Richard wanted Serena and her sisters to be intelligent, well-rounded people. Richard once said, "What do you do when you leave tennis? Assuming you live until you're seventy-five, you've got fifty years to be a fool."

Following their parents' lead, Serena and Venus always talked about the many exciting jobs they would have after tennis. As the years went by, both Serena and Venus certainly delivered on those promises. Many former critics of the Williams family now admit that, in **hindsight**, their father's careful approach appears to have been the right one all along.

Time For Some Help

By 1991, Venus had risen to be the top-ranked twelve-and-under player in Southern California, while Serena became the region's highest-ranked ten-year-old. Richard decided that his daughters had finally advanced to the point that they now needed professional instruction. After researching all the top coaches in the country, he selected well-known Rick Macci and his tennis academy in Haines City, Florida. Both sisters were offered tennis scholarships to the academy, and the entire Williams family moved to Florida.

The girls trained on and off with Macci for four years, from 1991 to 1995. Richard also tried other influential coaches during that time. At one point, Richard decided to have Serena and Venus attend the Nick Bollettieri Tennis Academy, which was bigger and which featured mental as well as physical training. However, the Bollettieri staff and the Williams family did not get along. The relationship lasted only six weeks before Serena and Venus moved back to Macci.

No matter who coached Serena and Venus, Richard continued to keep a firm grip on their careers. In tennis, players usually start in **juniors**, where they play with other children of similar age and skill. The USTA wanted Serena and Venus to play in more junior tournaments, and perhaps even turn professional, but once again their father refused. Instead, he insisted that they continue to improve their skills by practicing against better, stronger players, which usually meant male instructors.

Serena's parents had reason to be concerned about how tournaments and the professional tour could hurt their girls if they started too young.

Dangers for Young Players

When competing in tournaments, young players must be able to deal with the pressure of facing more experienced competitors who may be further advanced both mentally and physically. At the same

Jennifer Capriati flashes an infectious smile as a fourteen-year-old shortly after turning professional. However, facing so much pressure at such an early age hurt her career and served as a cautionary tale for the Williams sisters.

time, the young player also has to deal with strange places, tiresome travel, homesickness, boisterous crowds, and the demands of reporters and broadcasters. Richard knew that some young players had been pushed too far by their parents and coaches before they were ready, causing them to burn out and quit tennis.

Jennifer Capriati had turned professional in 1990 just before she turned fourteen. Like Serena and Venus, Capriati was coached by her father. She beat experienced women professionals at an early age. Capriati became overwhelmed by the pressure of winning tournaments, however. She began to make bad choices in her behavior, including being charged with shoplifting and with possession of marijuana, an illegal drug. Capriati became estranged from her father and decided to quit tennis when she was only eighteen. While she successfully returned to tennis years later and patched up things with her father, she continues to battle depression and drugs to this day, and many believe she missed her greatest years.

Unfortunately, Capriati's story is not the only sad one. Tracy Austin has spoken about difficulties she faced as a young teen superstar when she played at Wimbledon when she was only fourteen years old. Austin was extremely shy and fairly small, standing just four feet eleven inches (150 cm) and weighing just under 90 pounds (41 kg). Austin said that she was really still "a little girl. I didn't mature quickly, physically or emotionally … I found the press could be really hard. They asked me questions I had never thought about."

Pam Shriver turned pro at fifteen and the next year made it all the way to the finals at the US Open. The day after the match she faced the reality of going back to her high school classroom.

The 6-foot (1.8 meters) Shriver's career was held back by constant injuries, and she later said, "Now I know why it happened. I was a tall, skinny kid. I was a weak child, and I served too hard for my strength."

Other Concerns

Richard may have also been worried that his daughters would face racism. At the time, most tennis players were white, and only a small number of African American tennis players had ever managed to become successful professionals. Both Serena and Venus had already experienced instances of racism while playing in California, and their father worried that these situations might occur more often if they competed in larger tournaments where the stakes and the pressure would be even bigger.

While Macci disagreed with many of Richard's ideas, he went along with the plan. Sometimes the girls would practice less than one hour a day, and if their grades suffered in school, they would stop practicing altogether.

As Venus continued to get better, so did Serena. She was shorter than Venus; Serena would eventually reach five feet nine inches in height (175 cm) while Venus would grow to be 6 feet one inch (185 cm). However, Serena played with more control and precision. Sometimes Serena would bend against Venus's superior power, but she would never break. She began to occasionally beat Venus while continuing to develop the competitive, relentless style that would make her a champion.

Turning Pro

In 1994, fourteen-year-old Venus was gaining fame but still had not played in a major tournament. Turning professional could make it possible for Venus and Serena to earn large amounts of money from tournaments and **endorsements**. At the time, the professional Women's Tennis Association (**WTA**) was discussing a new rule that would limit the number of tournaments that players under eighteen could enter. Venus decided she wanted to turn professional before the new rule went into effect.

Richard remained opposed, but the Williams family eventually put the issue to a vote. Venus was allowed to turn pro with the understanding that she would continue to excel at her studies and limit her tournament play. Serena followed her sister and turned professional the following year.

Joining the World's Top Ten

Shortly after Venus turned professional, she signed a $12 million endorsement deal with Reebok that changed life for the entire Williams family. They soon moved to a 10-acre (4-hectare) estate in Palm Beach Gardens, Florida. The grounds included a tennis court as well as two small lakes. They had certainly come a long way from their start in Compton.

Even before Serena followed Venus as a professional, her father thought that she had a better feel for tennis than Venus and that she was more aggressive on the court. Richard believed that Serena would eventually eclipse Venus and become the best player in tennis, and he was not afraid to tell that to anyone who would listen.

By then, the WTA had put new rules in place, so fourteen-year-old Serena could not play in major tournaments. She did travel with Venus to her events, which helped Serena learn about the strengths and weaknesses of the other players. She also experienced how it would feel to compete in major tournaments and what the pressure would be like.

Opposite: Sixteen-year-old Serena Williams exults after she upset Monica Seles in the quarterfinals of the 1997 Ameritech Cup.

Serena was permitted to enter junior tournaments in Florida, and she proved to be a superior player. She had a 46–3 record on the United States Tennis Association junior tour and was ranked No. 1 in her age group in Florida.

Serena played her first professional tennis match, in a small tournament called the Belle Challenge, in November 1995 in Quebec, Canada. Unranked and relatively unknown, Serena lost. Those results would quickly change when Serena joined the women's professional tennis tour in 1997.

Intimidation or Racism?

In August 1997, Venus nearly won the US Open, the most important tennis tournament in the United States and one of the four major tennis championships in the world. After beating two **seeded** players, she lost in the final match to top-ranked Martina Hingis.

Richard and Oracene had always worried about racism on the tennis tour, and during that US Open tournament, the sensitive subject became a major issue for the Williams family. Her semi-final match pitted Venus against a strong player, eleventh-seeded Irina Spirlea of Romania. At one point while changing sides, Venus and Irina appeared to collide as they passed each other beside the net. Did Irina bump into Venus, or did Venus cause the contact? Was it on purpose, meant to intimidate the other player, or was it simply an accident?

After Venus won in an exciting **tiebreaker**, reporters asked Venus if she felt the bumping incident was related to the fact that she was black and Irina was white. Venus seemed genuinely surprised that anyone would even think to ask a question like that, and she said no.

Her father, however, had a different point of view. Richard Williams said that both Venus and Serena had faced racial prejudice on the pro tour because they were black. He also made disparaging comments about Spirlea that did nothing but heighten the tension over the matter. The subject of race, and how the Williams family fit within the tennis world, became an issue that is still is talked about today.

First Big Win

While her sister made a big splash in the 1997 US Open, Serena was also beginning to make a name for herself. In a tournament in Chicago, Serena played Mary Pierce, then the world's seventh-ranked player. Serena defeated Pierce in straight **sets** to make the quarterfinals.

Serena next played Monica Seles, the fourth-ranked player in the world. Serena lost the first set, 4-6, but she then fought back and won the next two sets, 6-1 and 6-1, to win the match. Serena became the lowest-ranked player ever to beat two top-ten players in the same tournament. Serena lost her semifinal match to Lindsay Davenport, but her impressive performance in the tournament helped her to jump in rank from number 304 to number 102. Serena managed to crack the top 100 by the end of the 1997 season.

Pam Shriver, a star herself, practiced with Serena in Chicago and was impressed by her skill and incredible strength. "Serena's forehand wasn't big on control," Shriver remembered, "but as far as power … wow! She was just cracking the ball." After losing to Serena, Monica Seles said, "She hit some great shots, and you have to attribute that to her being a great athlete."

Strangely, Serena attributes an accidental injury she suffered in December 1997 for helping her get even better at tennis. According to Serena, she fell off her skateboard and badly jammed her left wrist while reaching out to break her fall. She then aggravated the injury while practicing later that day.

Up until that time, Serena's favorite tennis stroke was her two-handed backhand, which she hit using both hands. Her weakest was her forehand, which she hit with her right hand. While she was hurt, Serena could not use her left arm to hit her backhand so she concentrated on hitting her forehand, which improved tremendously. When her left wrist healed, Serena could now hit powerful and effective strokes from either side.

Sister Versus Sister: Act One

Serena's quick climb up the ranks put her on a collision course with her sister. Given that Serena and Venus were close in age and were beginning to play at the highest levels of the sport, it was inevitable that they would eventually play each other. Although they had practiced together all their lives, competing head-to-head in a real match would be an entirely different experience for them.

In 1998, Serena and Venus won their first-round matches in the Australian Open, the first of four Grand Slam tournaments each year. Through the luck of the **draw,** they were then scheduled to oppose each other in the second round. This would be the first time they played each other as professionals, and the first time in history that two African American sisters competed against each other in any professional sports event.

Imagine the excitement as tennis fans anticipated the first meeting between these two sisters, African Americans raised in

Serena (*right*) and Venus Williams (*left*) salute the crowd after facing each other as professionals for the first time at the Australian Open in 1998.

the inner city, close in age and skill, publicized for years by their controversial father. Few realized at the time that this first Serena-versus-Venus contest would only mark the beginning of one the most intriguing and long-running rivalries in tennis history.

Venus won that first match, but the way both sisters reacted after it ended became an even bigger story. They met at the net, clasped hands, then turned and bowed together while the crowd roared. After the match, Venus told reporters that: "It wasn't fun eliminating my little sister, but I have to be tough. After the match, I said 'I'm sorry I had to take you out.' Since I am older, I have the feeling that I should win. I really wouldn't want to lose. But that's the only person I would be happy losing to because I would say, 'Go ahead, Serena. Take the title.'"

Serena was equally complimentary of her sister. "If I had to lose in the second round, there's no one better to lose to than Venus," Serena said.

Serena and Venus played each other for a second time that year in May at the Italian Open. Venus won that match as well, but neither sister played well. Some fans and reporters thought that the sisters did not play as hard against each other as they did against other opponents, perhaps trying to protect the other from having to lose. Others believed that facing someone they were so close to emotionally made it difficult to play their best. Serena and Venus dismissed the speculation, saying that they tried to win every match no matter who they were playing. It was clear, though, that they played each other differently than they played other opponents.

United in Doubles

They may have disliked facing each other across the net, but Serena and Venus loved playing as a team. Major tournaments feature singles matches as well as doubles, when two players team up against another pair. Many players enter both the singles and the doubles competition in the same tournament. Serena and Venus relished the opportunity to partner together in doubles matches, which allowed them to combine their skills and familiarity with each other's style to dominate their opponents. In 1998, they won four women's doubles titles. Serena also won mixed doubles titles with male partner Max Mirnyi at Wimbledon and the US Open.

Early in 1999, Richard felt that his daughters were on the cusp of greatness, but he worried that they could become distracted if they played against each other too much. He decided to avoid the situation whenever possible by preventing them from entering the same tournaments except for Grand Slam events.

The strategy worked. In March, Serena won the final in a tournament in Paris, her first win on the WTA tour. Later that same day, Venus won in Oklahoma City, marking the first time that two sisters won singles championships in two different tennis tournaments on the same day.

Later that same month, Serena played in the Evert Cup in Indian Wells, California and won the singles title, defeating top players including Mary Pierce, Lindsay Davenport, and Steffi Graf. Serena had now won eleven matches in a row, and her Evert Cup prize winnings totaled $200,000.

Next on the tournament agenda was the Lipton Championship in Miami, which Serena and Venus both entered. This is one of the most important tournaments for men and women outside of the majors. Serena made the finals when she beat the top-ranked Hingis in straight sets, increasing her match-winning streak to sixteen. Venus defeated Steffi Graf to also make the finals, once again setting up a sister-against-sister contest for the championship.

The Williams Show

As the match began, Richard Williams held up a message board on which he had written "Welcome to the Williams Show." Each

Coach, Manager, and Father

Serena credits her father for making her the player she is today. In her 2009 autobiography, Serena wrote, "This book is dedicated to my Daddy. Your vision and undying dedication made everything I do possible. I love you."

Richard Williams holds up a sign that reads "Welcome to the Williams Show" at the finals of the Lipton Championships in 1999.

Richard Williams's methods were certainly unorthodox. After teaching himself to play tennis by relying on books and videos and by observing other players, he insisted on teaching Serena and Venus himself rather than relying on coaches. He limited their schedules, insisted that they pursue other interests, and managed their affairs. He also loved to speak out in public, predicting stardom for his daughters, bragging about their skill, and openly talking about racism on the tennis tour.

Serena realizes that, even today, her father remains a controversial figure in women's tennis. "Say what you will about my Dad (and folks have said an awful lot over the years)," she wrote, "[but] he had a gentle demeanor when he wanted to, especially when we were first starting out … After every loss, he'd offer a word of encouragement, a point of praise."

Speaking about her father's importance in her career, Serena said, "My Dad—I think there is a very thin line between being a manager and being a coach and being a dad. That's three different roles that, fortunately, my Dad was able to do well. As a manager, I think he's the best. He produced Venus and Serena Williams, so what better can you do? Not only one champion, but two."

sister tried to blow the other off the court. Venus won the first set in dominating fashion, 6-1, but Serena came back to win the second set, 6-4. The third and deciding set was close, but in the end Venus prevailed, 6-4. Venus had won again.

Both sisters were subdued after the match ended. Clearly, playing each other with the title on the line was not something they enjoyed. "When you play an opponent who knows exactly what you are going to do, it's going to be tough," Serena said at the time. But she wasn't angry. "Family comes first, no matter how many times we play each other. Nothing will come between me and my sister."

The final major tournament of the year is the US Open, and it is held in late summer. The 1999 schedule placed Serena and Venus in opposite ends of the draw, which meant that they would not play each other unless each sister made it through to the tournament final. With the confidence that Richard and Oracene had instilled in them, the sisters boldly predicted that they would meet for the championship.

The pressure to win in tennis can be enormous even under normal circumstances. By publicly predicting their own success, Serena and Venus drew even more attention to themselves, and that served to raise the tension even higher. The publicity surrounding their matches affected their opponents as well. Instead of being questioned about their own games or chances for success, other players were asked what they thought of the Williams sisters and how they would fare against them. Some players, already frustrated at the attention that the Williams sisters commanded, tried to avoid the controversy, but others were happy to react.

Martina Hingis was the top-ranked woman at the time and favored to win the championship. After facing so many questions

Serena Williams defeated top-ranked Martina Hingis for the US Open Championship in 1999. It was her first Grand Slam victory.

about Serena, Venus, and their father, Hingis finally lost patience and responded that everyone in the Williams family had "a big mouth." Serena fired back and accused Hingis, who had not graduated from high school, of not benefiting from a "formal education."

Unexpectedly, and perhaps staged by the WTA, Richard Williams stepped into the fray and tried to calm the situation. He said that he loved Martina and that one of the things he wanted the most was to get her autograph. Hingis accepted the peace offering and presented Richard Williams with a signed T-shirt. She also gave him a big kiss on the cheek while photographers covering the event snapped away.

Serena was seeded seventh in the tournament rankings. With everyone's attention back on tennis, both Serena and Venus made it to the quarterfinals. After being down one set against Monica Seles, Serena rallied to move on to the semifinals. After the match, Serena told reporters that if she continued to play as well as she did against Seles, no one else could beat her.

Lindsay Davenport had other ideas. Davenport was at that time the world's second-ranked women's tennis player, and she was one of the few women who was bigger and stronger than Serena. The six foot two inch (188 cm) Davenport may have thought that she could overpower Serena, but this is where Serena's years of experience competing against her taller sister would play to her advantage.

Davenport began the match by aggressively attacking Serena, but Serena responded with just as much force. After Serena took the first set, Davenport came back to win the second, extending the match into a decisive third set. In the end, Serena triumphed and moved into the semifinals.

Unfortunately for the Williams sisters, Martina Hingis had managed to defeat Venus in a close and exhausting three-set match, meaning that she, and not Venus, would oppose Serena in the final. Venus was bitterly disappointed about not moving on to play Serena for the championship. After Venus lost, Serena said, "I've never seen her that down before."

First Grand Slam!

Although Venus had been eliminated, she may have done Serena a tremendous favor by extending Hingis in such a tough contest. As the championship match began, Serena seemed to have more energy and confidence than Hingis. She won the first set 6-3. Hingis managed to recover and force the second set to a tiebreaker, but Serena outlasted her and won the match in straight sets. At the age of seventeen, two weeks before her eighteenth birthday, Serena Williams had won the US Open Women's championship. It was her first Grand Slam singles title and the first for the Williams family.

Serena screamed with joy after winning the final point, and tears streamed down her face. After the match, Serena said "I thought, 'Should I scream, should I yell, or should I cry?' I guess I ended up doing them all!"

Years later, Serena still clearly remembered winning that first Grand Slam.

I'll never forget my Dad said, "This is the moment we have been working for all our lives. Stay focused and take your chances, and don't be afraid." And I really took that conversation to heart ... I always said that match changed my life and my career. I remember thinking, "I gotta go for it" ... and I said "Serena, if you don't go for it now, you'll regret it for the rest of your life. Even if you miss, you just gotta go for it." And she

Venus Williams congratulates her sister after Serena beat her for the first time in a tournament final, in Munich, Germany, in 1999.

served the ball and I remember I hit a forehand as hard as I could down the line. And [after winning the point] that kind of set the foundation for the rest of my career, was just going for it.

Serena's job wasn't finished after she won the singles championship. She and sister Venus had also advanced to the women's doubles final, and the match was due to take place later that same day. They both had trouble focusing during the first set and lost, but they were able to bounce back and dominate the rest of the match and win the title.

Later that year, Serena and Venus reached the finals of the Grand Slam Cup tournament in Munich, Germany. There, for the first time, Serena managed to finally defeat her sister in a professional match. It took three sets, but in the end Serena triumphed, 6-1, 3-6, 6-3. "She knew eventually I would take a match from her," Serena said.

President Bill Clinton remembered seeing Serena play that year. He said, "Serena was only seventeen at the time, and she just gave this aura out, that … once she mastered her power, no one in the world would be able to beat her."

At the end of 1999, Serena finished ranked number four in the world, only one spot below her sister. She was now on her way to greatness.

Chapter 3

Injuries, Rivalries, and Triumph

Serena began the 2000 season battling health issues. First, she injured a ligament in her right knee in February. Later that spring, she hurt her left foot.

Serena's health finally improved by the time Wimbledon began late in June. She and Venus advanced to face each other in the semifinals. As the sisters prepared for their match, everyone looked for signs of envy or conflict between them. Serena had already won a Grand Slam title; her older sister Venus had not. Was Venus jealous? How did their parents feel?

A First for Venus

As it turned out, both Richard and Oracene were not at all comfortable seeing their daughters compete against each other. Neither parent attended the match. Richard paced the grounds outside the stands, while Oracene traveled back to Florida to watch on television.

Opposite: Serena and Venus Williams celebrate after winning the Women's Doubles Gold Medal at the 2000 Olympic Games in Sydney, Australia.

The match began with both sisters playing tentatively, missing shots that they'd usually make with ease. Even the crowd seemed more quiet than normal, with many unsure whom to cheer for. In the end, Venus beat Serena, 6-2, 7-6, with Serena uncharacteristically serving a double **fault** on **match point** to hand Venus the victory. Serena was visibly upset after the loss, and Venus downplayed her own celebration while trying to console Serena after the match.

Venus then went on to defeat Lindsay Davenport in the Wimbledon final and win her own first Grand Slam championship. Serena proved that she was not upset with her sister when, the following day, she teamed with Venus to capture the Wimbledon doubles title.

The following September, Serena and Venus won the Olympic doubles gold medal in Sydney, Australia, while Venus also won the gold in singles.

Serena was proud of her sister's success, but she remained a fierce competitor and vowed to improve to keep pace with her older sister's rise. In January 2001, Serena told a reporter that she wanted to become the best women's tennis player in the world. "I am determined to take my game to a new level this year," she said. "I have done well, but professionally, not as well as I would like. I see myself as doing so much better … I really want to get to the top."

The year did not start as well as Serena hoped. She lost in the quarterfinals at the Australian Open after suffering food poisoning before a match, but she did team with Venus to win their first Australian Open doubles title. Her difficulties in Australia were nothing, however, compared to what Serena would soon encounter at Indian Wells.

A Disturbing Experience

The Indian Wells Masters tournament takes place each March in
a small town outside of Palm Springs, California. Serena won the
tournament in 1999, and it became one of her favorite events. In her
autobiography, Serena wrote, "I loved the setting … I loved that the
fans were knowledgeable and respectful and appreciative." Indian
Wells was close enough to Los Angeles that the entire Williams/
Price family could attend. "We'd all stay together in the hotel and
hang out, and it was so much fun," Serena remembered.

In 2001, both Serena and Venus advanced through the
tournament and were scheduled to meet in the semifinals.
The crowd anticipated a great match between the two famous,
homegrown sisters. However, Venus struggled with the heat in her
previous match, and she also complained about injuring her knee.
Just minutes before Serena and Venus were scheduled to play, the
tournament announced that Venus was withdrawing, allowing
Serena a free pass to the final.

The circumstances of Venus's withdrawal remain controversial
to this day. The Williams family claims that Venus discussed her
exhaustion and knee problems with tournament directors well in
advance, but the officials wanted the match to go on and refused
to either postpone it or announce that Venus would withdraw
until the last moment. Others believe that the Williams family
staged the injury and that Venus purposely defaulted so that Serena
could advance.

Regardless of the circumstances, Serena moved on to play a
Belgian woman, Kim Clijsters, in the final. What happened next

Venus and Richard Williams comfort Serena after she won the championship at Indian Wells in 2001 despite enduring jeers from a hostile crowd.

Serena Williams: Setting New Standards

still haunts tennis today as one of the ugliest incidents in its history. Selena Roberts, a reporter for the *New York Times*, described the scene as the crowd raged against the entire Williams family:

> About five minutes before the match, a sun-kissed crowd known for its relaxed spirit spotted Richard and Venus Williams beginning a long walk down the 50 steps to their courtside perch. Immediately, a crescendo of boos began ushering the father and daughter to their seats … Halfway to his destination, a defiant Richard Williams turned and shook his fist at his 15,000 critics … Few wanted to forgive Venus Williams for pulling out of her semifinal against her sister four minutes before the match on Thursday night … Few wanted to believe that her exit was not part of a fix conjured up by their father. … Once Richard and Venus sat down, Serena Williams had to absorb the brunt of the fury. Her double faults became reason for celebration. Her shots into the net ignited cheers. But Serena Williams eventually channeled her frayed emotions into her game to take the title, 4-6, 6-4, 6-2.

"At first, obviously, I wasn't happy," Serena Williams said. "I don't think mentally I was ready for that. To be honest, what I literally did on a changeover, I prayed to God to help me be strong, not even to win, but to be strong, not listen to the crowd."

On her last emotional swing of the match, Williams punched a forehand crosscourt for a winner. The celebration was awkward. As she began to wave to the crowd, boos mixed with a smattering of applause. "I'd like to thank everyone who supported me, and if you didn't, I love you guys anyway," Williams said after accepting her trophy and a winner's check for $330,000.

After the match, Serena said that someone in the crowd called her a racist term. Her father Richard also claimed that he and the rest of the family endured racist comments from those seated nearby. While the crowd may have simply been frustrated by not seeing Serena and Venus play each other, others thought race may have played a role as well. Hearing the crowd cheer for a Belgian player, a British commentator remarked, "An American crowd booing an American family, and you'd have to say that it smacks a little bit of racism."

Venus proudly complimented her sister for winning the title in the face of such difficulty. "Well, she won the match because she is a champion. She has the heart of a tiger. Have you seen *Rocky* [the movie]? Well, that's her."

After the tournament, Serena vowed never to return to Indian Wells. She said, "The title will go on without me, but I'm not going back. … You look back at people like Martin Luther King, and Malcolm X, and Rosa Parks. If they didn't believe, and stand up for what they believe in, then we wouldn't have the freedoms that we experience today. What I had to go through was so small compared to what they had to go through. And if I can't stand up for something like this then, who am I? What have they taught me in history?"

Serena kept her word and did not return to play at Indian Wells until 2015. When she finally agreed to go back, Serena said, "I was raised by my mom to love and forgive freely … I have faith that fans at Indian Wells have grown with the game and know me better than they did in 2001. Indian Wells was a pivotal moment of my story, and I am a part of the tournament's story as well. Together, we have a chance to write a different ending."

Serena faced more health issues after Indian Wells. Knee injuries, fatigue, and the flu dogged her until that August, when she returned to form with a victory over Jennifer Capriati in the Rogers AT&T Cup in Toronto. Serena's return to the winners column served as a precursor for what was to come next, the 2001 US Open.

A Williams Grand Slam Final

Late that summer, Serena and Venus powered through their respective **brackets** at the US Open to meet in the final. This would mark the first time they'd play each other for a Grand Slam title.

The all-Williams final represented another first. Interest in the match ran so high that, tennis fan or not, everyone was talking about the African American sisters who would battle for supremacy at the US Open. The tournament and the TV network televising the match decided to change their schedule, moving the championship from Saturday afternoon to the evening so that more people could watch it live.

On September 8, 2001, US television broadcast Serena against Venus at night, in prime time. John McEnroe, former tennis champion and TV commentator for the match, said on-air that, "This is a great night for tennis in general. And I think the only thing more unbelievable than the women playing in prime time is the Williams story itself. "

For the Williams family, the pressure that night was even more difficult than usual. Sister Isha Price said, "It was a very tense and hard thing to watch. It's stressful to watch them play because you want them both to win. You feel there's a little guilt, like, OK, you can't clap for Serena, you can't clap for Venus."

In the end, older sister Venus defeated her younger sister, 6-2, 6-4, winning her second US Open and her fourth Grand Slam. More than twenty-two million people watched on television that night, fifty per cent more than had watched the Women's US Open final the previous year.

While Serena may have lost the 2001 US Open to her sister, her strong performance was a sign of things to come. In 2002, Serena and Venus would together dominate women's tennis and oppose each other in three straight Grand Slam finals.

Early in 2002, Serena advanced to the finals at the German Open in Berlin and then won her next tournament, the Italian Open in Rome. Her performance took on even more importance because both tournaments were played on clay.

Different Surfaces, Different Games

Tennis can be played on many different types of surfaces—clay, grass, and what are called hard courts. The court surface has a major effect on the way the game is played and the type of player who is successful.

Clay courts consist of crushed shale, stone, or brick. Clay tends to slow the speed of the ball and produce higher bounces, which hurts players who depend on hard serves and powerful strokes. Grass courts are very fast, with low bounces and short, quick points that benefit hard hitters. Hard courts are made of smooth, rigid material and feature consistent bounces and firm footing. Hard courts can vary from one location to the next and are generally faster than clay but slower than grass.

After winning on a clay surface in the Italian Open, Serena Williams entered the 2002 French Open brimming with confidence.

Injuries, Rivalries, and Triumph

Serena Williams holds the championship trophy after defeating Venus for the French Open title in 2002.

The four Grand Slam tournaments feature different surfaces. Roland Garros (the official name of the French Open) is played on clay; Wimbledon is on grass. The Australian and US Opens both use hard surfaces, but different types. Some players have an advantage in certain tournaments, based on their strengths and how they play.

When Serena won the Italian Open, she considered it more than just another victory. It was her first victory on a clay surface, and it boosted her confidence as she prepared for the French Open. "A lot of people insist I am not a clay-court player, although I am," she told the *New York Times*. "So it makes me feel good, especially going into Roland Garros."

A few days later, Serena spoke with the *Times* by phone about her growing confidence and compared herself to her sister. "I think nowadays I am very focused. I don't believe many people can beat me, if any," she said. "I just think now if I play well, it's hard to overcome me. I think Venus has had that attitude for a long while. Now, I've been able to develop it."

Three Slams to the Top

Serena and Venus both made it to the finals of the French Open. When Serena won the title, it was the first time she had beaten her sister in a Grand Slam match. After winning, Serena told *Tennis* magazine, "To finally win a match against Venus in a big tournament was a pretty big confidence booster. I learned that it's OK to do well against your sister." For her part, Venus said, "I want to win, but I want Serena to win also … My goal has always been to be number one in the world, but not to take the number-one ranking from my sister."

Following the French Open, Serena's rank rose to number two in the world, just below Venus, who had risen to the top spot just

Serena's Biggest Rivals

As of early 2017, Serena Williams had played professional tennis for more than twenty years, competing against all the best players over that time. So who does Serena consider to be her greatest rival?

When asked the question in 2015, Serena paused and then answered, "Okay. I have played a lot of people ... Let me think. I'm starting in the '90s and thinking in the '90s and then 2000s. It's so hard to say. I have played so many great players from Hingis to Davenport, Monica, Steffi. I have played some unbelievably tough players.""

Serena Williams named Martina Hingis as one of her top opponents all-time, but her sister Venus may actually be Serena's greatest rival.

Serena eventually named four players: Lindsay Davenport, Martina Hingis, Steffi Graf, and Monica Seles. Serena won ten of fourteen matches against Davenport and four of five against Seles. Graf retired shortly after Serena turned professional, and they played only twice, splitting their matches, 1-1. Hingis played well against Serena, but Serena still holds a 7-6 edge.

In truth, however, Serena's greatest rival may be her sister Venus. After their match in the final of the 2017 Australian Open, they had opposed each other twenty-eight times, with Serena holding a seventeen to eleven advantage. Their matches included fifteen Grand Slam contests, of which nine were championship matches (Serena won seven, including their 2017 meeting in Australia), and eleven other tournament finals. Beginning with the 2002 French Open, they appeared in four consecutive Grand Slam singles finals, the first time in the **open era** that the same two players fought for a Grand Slam title four straight times.

Back in 1997, Venus Williams predicted, "My greatest rival will be my sister." Twenty years later, she may have been right.

three months earlier in February. For the first time in history, sisters held the top two positions in tennis. Their accomplishment fulfilled what their father had predicted many years before, that his daughters would rise to be the two highest-ranked tennis players in the world.

That July again brought the challenge of Wimbledon. Once again, Serena and Venus won all their matches and were pitted against each other for the championship, the third time in the last four Grand Slams that they would compete for the title. Serena won, 7-6, 6-3, to capture her third Grand Slam title and her second in a row over her sister. They then teamed to win the Wimbledon doubles title as well. Serena's victory allowed her to finally claim the number one female ranking in tennis, passing her sister.

The following September, Serena and Venus made it three straight all-sister Grand Slam finals when they advanced to meet in the championship match at the US Open. And, also for the third consecutive time, Serena defeated her sister for the crown.

Only six other women had ever won three Grand Slams in a row in the same year. Serena had missed the first Grand Slam of the year—the Australian Open—due to an injury, but her victories at Roland Garros, Wimbledon, and the US Open allowed her to claim the "Surface Slam" (three straight Slam victories on three different surfaces—clay, grass, and hard court). Williams finished 2002 with a 56–5 won-loss record, eight singles titles, and the world number one ranking.

Accolades, Yet Criticism

The Serena-versus-Venus story continued to intrigue people who were not even interested in tennis. Praise for Serena and Venus was not unanimous, however.

Some in tennis feared that fans might lose interest if the same two players dominated every major tournament. Others thought that neither sister played to her full capabilities when matched against the other, either because they were intimidated or they wanted to protect their sister. Rumors continued to circulate that the Williams family had constructed a master plan to make sure that both Serena and Venus shared the tennis spotlight, and that they secretly plotted in advance to choose who won any particular match.

In retrospect, these accusations seem ludicrous. First, both Serena and Venus had to win all of their matches in a tournament before they got the chance to play each other, and their opponents were certainly not going to cooperate and let Serena or Venus beat them. Second, the record shows that, when the sisters did play each other, there was no pattern to who won or lost, and the loser always appeared unhappy in defeat while still graciously congratulating her winning sister.

The Streak Ends

After claiming the US Open, Serena continued her winning ways, taking titles in two more tournaments. Kim Clijsters finally ended Serena's eighteen-match winning streak when she managed to defeat Serena late in the year in the final of the WTA Tour Championships in Los Angeles.

The year 2002 turned out to be fantastic for Serena professionally. She became the top-ranked woman, she captured three of the four Grand Slams, and she won fifty-six out of sixty-one matches and eight of thirteen tournaments she entered. Her

Although divorced, both Oracene Price and Richard Williams still attend their daughters' tennis matches and play major roles in their lives.

accomplishments led to her being named the Female Athlete of the Year by the Associated Press (AP).

The year also brought some sadness, however. Richard and Oracene separated and later divorced. Oracene then dropped the Williams name and returned to her maiden name, Price. Although they were no longer together, Oracene and Richard continued to support Serena and Venus. Oracene continues to attend many matches today, often sitting in the family box with daughter Isha.

The Serena Slam

Serena and Venus Williams began 2003 with more of the same. Both sisters made it to the final of the Australian Open, the first

Grand Slam of the year. It was the first time that either Serena or Venus had advanced to the Australian Open final and the fourth time in a row that the sisters would play each other for a Grand Slam title. Continuing her recent dominance, Serena beat her sister for the fourth consecutive time in a Slam final event, winning, 7-6, 3-6, 6-4.

Serena became only one of five women to hold the titles for all four Grand Slam events at one time, and the first to do it since Steffi Graf in 1994. Her victory also introduced a bit of controversy, however.

Serena had won four Grand Slam titles in a row, but she did not win them consecutively (Australian, French, Wimbledon and US Open) in the same calendar year. People began to refer to her accomplishment as the "Serena Slam," which meant four consecutive slam titles regardless of the order and the year.

At the 2003 French Open, Serena lost to Justine Henin-Hardenne, but she exacted some revenge by defeating Henin-Hardenne easily in the Wimbledon semifinals. Venus also made the finals, but she had injured her stomach muscles and was not at full strength as Serena defeated her again, Serena's sixth Grand Slam title.

Unfortunately the injury bug caught up to Serena as well when she reinjured her left knee. Serena tried to play through her pain, but she eventually realized that she risked further injury and decided to undergo surgery in August 2003, preventing her from entering the US Open.

At first, Serena claimed that the injury occurred while she was playing tennis. In her 2009 biography, however, she revealed that she actually hurt her knee while dancing in high-heeled shoes at a club in Los Angeles. "The first major injury of my career, and it happened on the dance floor," Serena wrote. "I hated being sidelined for such a frivolous thing. It was embarrassing—so much so that I couldn't bring myself to tell anyone how it happened."

While taking time off to recover, Serena pursued some of her interests outside tennis, including acting and fashion. When her Puma endorsement deal expired, Serena received millions of dollars to sign with Nike, and she appeared in Nike's "What If?" commercials as a beach volleyball player.

When critics accused Serena of being more focused on outside activities like fashion, acting, and modeling than on tennis, she defended her choices. "I like that stuff. How many twenty-one-year-olds are making the living I'm making, getting to do the things that I do? ... I'm not afraid to be in the public eye. That's just me."

A Family Tragedy

Shortly after her surgery, Serena and her family suffered a terrible tragedy that made tennis wins and losses seem insignificant.

On September 14, 2003, Yetunde Price, the oldest of the five Williams sisters, was shot and killed while sitting in a car during a confrontation with a group of people in Compton. Yetunde was thirty-one and had three children.

The news of Yetunde's death crushed Serena and the rest of the Williams family. "She was almost like a mom to me, Venus, and Lyn," Serena wrote afterwards. Serena had been spending even more time with Yetunde since her injury, and she later admitted that it took her a long time to recover from her sister's death. "Tennis was about the last thing on my mind, just then. Forget that I wasn't physically ready to pick up a racket. It just didn't seem all that important."

Dealing with her sister's murder, her own injury, and outside interests caused Serena to miss many months of tennis in 2003. She

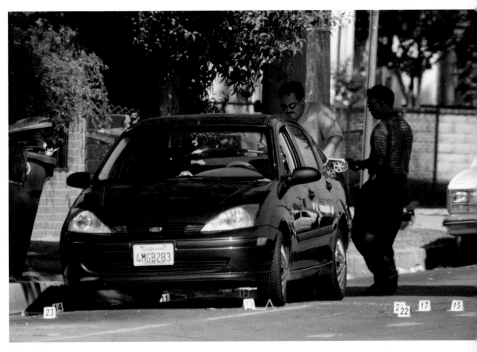

Serena's oldest sister Yetunde Price was fatally shot at this spot in September 2003. Yetunde's tragic murder affected Serena for years afterward.

lost her number-one ranking to Kim Clijsters after holding it for fifty-seven consecutive weeks. Eventually, Serena realized that she needed to get back to work and return to tennis. She succeeded, if only for a short time.

High Fashion

Ever since Serena first appeared on a tennis court, she wanted to display her sense of fashion and style as much as her tennis talent. The year 2004 stands out as much for her fashion statements as for her uneven tennis performance.

Serena won her first tournament in Florida early in 2004, but she could not sustain her high level of play at the French Open. Even

Serena Williams wears her famous hip-hop outfit during the 2004 US Open.
Serena became known as much for her tennis outfits as for her play.

though she lost, Serena proved once again at Roland Garros that she was much more than just a tennis player, drawing attention by appearing in a fuchsia outfit with a bare midriff, a diamond-pierced bellybutton and a red flower in her hair.

Serena did raise her play that summer at Wimbledon, but she lost in the finals in a surprising upset to seventeen-year-old rising star Maria Sharapova. Some observers, including other players, felt that the Wimbledon loss helped to strip away the aura of invincibility that surrounded Serena after she had dominated tennis for several years.

Following Wimbledon, Serena's knee problems returned, and she had to withdraw from the Olympics. She returned for the US Open and, again, commanded attention as much for what she wore as how she played. Serena appeared in what became one of her most talked-about outfits. It featured a hip-hop look and included a studded sport tank, a short, denim skirt and, perhaps most famously, shiny black warm-up boots that fit over her sneakers. While her look was memorable, her game was anything but, and she lost to Jennifer Capriati in the quarterfinals.

In retrospect, Serena's return from her injury and her grief would prove to be more difficult than anyone expected. The next year would include its share of ups and downs, but it would take more time, and some real soul searching, before Serena would fully recover, return to form, and dominate.

Chapter 4

Self-Reflection and Rebirth

As the 2005 season began, tennis experts speculated that Serena was past her prime and that she would never dominate the tour as she had in the past. Jelena Dokic, another leading player, told BBC Sports, "That story is over. I don't even hear comments about Serena anymore."

Serena had other ideas, and she didn't wait long to prove the naysayers wrong. That January, at the Australian Open, Serena surprised everyone by soundly defeating Maria Sharapova in the semifinals and Lindsay Davenport in the finals to win her seventh Grand Slam singles title.

After her quick start, however, Serena could not sustain her early promise. That March, Venus beat Serena in a match, her first win over Serena after six straight losses. Serena did not play in the French Open due to an ankle injury. At Wimbledon, she lost in a surprise third-round upset to a player named Jill Craybas. Venus avenged her sister by later beating Craybas on her way to the singles title, winning her first Grand Slam since 2001. Venus defeated Serena again at the US Open that September.

Opposite: Serena shows her frustration while losing at Wimbledon in 2005 to a relatively unknown player, Jill Craybas.

In her 2009 autobiography, Serena admitted that she continued to mourn her sister during the 2005 season, nearly two years after Yetunde's death.

> My drive, my sense of mission and purpose, my desire to be the best in the world ... all those things had fallen away without me fully realizing it, and it wasn't clear if I'd ever get them back ... I was slipping into a depression ... it was an aching sadness, an [all over] weariness, a sudden disinterest in the world around me—in tennis, above all.

Struggling with her emotions as well as continued physical issues, Serena entered the Australian Open in January 2006 hoping to defend her 2005 title and start the year fresh. In the third round, however, she played poorly and lost in straight sets. After the match, she wrote, "I still remember walking to the players' locker room ... feeling so completely lost and beaten and confused."

A Life-Altering Experience

Serena went back home to Los Angeles and avoided picking up a tennis racket for months, skipping the French Open and Wimbledon. That summer, urged on by her family, Serena decided to begin counseling sessions, and the therapy she received helped her to start thinking about her life more positively. She also traveled to Africa for the first time. During her trip she visited Gorée Island, a location just off the coast of Senegal where slaves had once been assembled and forcibly sent to America and the Caribbean. She also spent time in Ghana, where she aided efforts to protect children from malaria.

Serena Williams chats with children during her visit to Africa in 2006, a trip that she later said changed her life.

Afterward, Serena told *People* magazine that her visit "just changed me. It gave me strength and courage, and let me know that I can endure anything." Seeing the suffering of children helped her to focus on life beyond tennis and made her want to help others. "The kids were so gorgeous, it broke my heart. Now I'm just trying to get other people to realize what's going on there."

Serena began to feel better, both physically and emotionally. She also regained her passion for tennis, writing in her biography:

> When I was a kid, I'd never made an active or conscious choice where tennis was concerned. It was always like tennis chose me. Don't get me wrong, I was honored to have been chosen, and I was blessed with a God-given gift ... But it had always been handed to me, and expected of me, and held out like a given ... It took reaching for it here, when I was down and desperate, for me to fully embrace the game. I chose tennis. At last.

Feeling a sense of renewal, Serena returned to the tennis tour and played in the US Open that September. Though she lost in the first round, her therapy, her trip to Africa, and the soul-searching she went through toward the end of 2006 set the stage for Serena's impressive climb back to the top spot in tennis.

Comeback

By 2007, Serena had nearly fallen out of the top one hundred of the rankings. She was determined to rise to number one again and said so, causing former men's Wimbledon winner and tennis commentator Pat Cash to call the idea "deluded." Serena entered the Australian Open, a tournament she had already won twice, as an unseeded player. People criticized her for being out of shape and unfocused, and Nike made it clear that the company might end her endorsement deal if she did not perform well. Talk about pressure!

Undeterred, Serena absolutely dominated her first match, losing only three games, and she defeated her next opponent in straight sets. She won her next four matches as well, twice fighting back after teetering only two points away from elimination. Serena had unexpectedly reached the final and would be playing Maria Sharapova, who was heavily favored to win.

Before the championship match, former player and television analyst Tracy Austin suggested that Serena had played a great tournament, but the "ride was over" and that Sharapova would have no trouble winning. Serena heard about the comments, and she thought that Austin''s remarks were mean and unnecessary. She decided to combine all the negative comments—about her weight, her preparation, and her chances, as well as the pressure from her sponsor Nike—and, as she said afterward, "mash them into one big positive."

Serena came out on fire and dominated Sharapova, losing just three games in a match that lasted just over one hour. The BBC called her performance "arguably the most powerful display ever seen in women's tennis." Serena was so excited after winning match point that she rolled on her back and kicked her legs into the air in celebration. She then addressed the cheering crowd and dedicated her win to her late sister Yetunde, saying "I would like to dedicate this win to my sister, who's not here. Her name is Yetunde. I just love her so much. So thanks, Tunde [her nickname]."

Serena's victory represented her first tournament win since the 2005 Australian Open, two full years earlier. Serena quickly rose to number fourteen in the rankings. After suffering more injuries to her thumb and knee, however, Serena did not win any more tournaments in 2007.

The Sisters Battle, Again

The following year started slowly when Serena failed to defend her Australian Open title, losing in the quarterfinals. Wimbledon would tell a different tale, however. Serena and Venus both advanced to the final, pitting the two sisters in a Grand Slam championship match for the seventh time. The games were close, but Serena struggled with her serve and Venus triumphed, 7-5, 6-4. Again, the winner's joy was muted by the fact that Venus had beaten her sister.

Serena Williams rejoices after defeating Maria Sharapova for the 2007
Australian Open singles title, which she dedicated to her sister, Yetunde.

Self-Reflection and Rebirth

Serena felt better after she teamed with Venus to win the doubles title, their third combined Wimbledon title and their seventh doubles title in a Grand Slam tournament. Later that summer, Serena joined Venus to win Olympic gold in doubles at Beijing, China.

In September, Serena defeated Venus on her way to her third US Open championship, her ninth Grand Slam singles title. Many people thought this match between the sisters was the best they ever played against each other, with both sets decided by tiebreakers, 7-6, 7-6. The victory helped Serena regain the world's number-one ranking for the first time since 2003.

After a successful 2008 season that included more than forty match victories, Serena said, "That was my goal, to be more consistent, to play more tournaments. I love playing tennis and love the competition and love being out there." However, Serena accomplished more that year than just regaining tennis dominance. In August, she started the Serena Williams Foundation to help young people be able to afford college. That November, she established the Serena Williams Secondary School in Kenya, Africa.

In 2009 Serena cemented her number-one ranking with singles wins in both the Australian Open and Wimbledon, with Serena once again defeating Venus in the Wimbledon final. She now held eleven Grand Slam singles titles.

Emotions Unchecked

Unfortunately, Serena's 2009 season is remembered for something more than her two Grand Slam titles. Late that summer at the US Open, Serena and Kim Clijsters were battling in a close match. During a crucial point, the line judge called a foot fault, ruling that

Serena's foot crossed the line during her serve. This is an uncommon call in tennis, and it caused her to lose the point. Serena erupted with an angry outburst, directing obscene language and threats at the official. Not only did Serena lose the match, she was fined a record amount and put on **probation**. Serena's reputation suffered a setback due to her sudden and unexpected loss of control.

Despite the incident at the US Open, 2009 still represented a spectacular year for Serena. The Associated Press named her its Female Athlete of the Year, and Stacey Allaster of the Women's Tennis Association wrote that, "We can attribute the strength and the growth of women's tennis … a great deal to her. She is a superstar." She continued her winning ways in 2010.

That January, Serena once again won the Australian Open, defending her title from the year before. She then duplicated the feat, defending her Wimbledon title for yet another Grand Slam win, giving her five of the past eight Slam singles titles. After that victory, Serena held up all ten fingers to the crowd, then closed her hands and extended three more fingers in the air, wiggling them to signify that she now had won thirteen Grand Slam singles events. Her triumph vaulted her past tennis legend Billie Jean King into sixth place among all female Grand Slam singles winners.

When asked where Serena ranked all time in women's tennis, former champion Martina Navratilova immediately answered, "Top five. It's not just about how many Slams you win or how many tournaments you win—it's just your game overall. And she's definitely got all the goods. It would have been fun to play her, but at the same time, I'm glad that I didn't have to."

That July, Serena severed a tendon in her foot when she stepped on broken glass in a restaurant, an injury that caused her to miss the

Praise From Opponents Past and Present

Many of Serena's former and current opponents marvel at her continued ability to compete, and win, on the tennis tour.

Martina Hingis, still an active doubles player in 2016 but retired from singles competition since 2007, called Serena "a phenomenal player. More than that, she's a phenomenon ... What's so important with a player like Serena is that she stays hungry and motivated and is able to play at the highest level."

Twenty-four-year-old Christina McHale has played Serena Williams three times in her young career. McHale lost all three, although she did win one tiebreaker against Serena in 2016 at Wimbledon. McHale recently wrote a column for the *Players Tribune* website in which she discussed her top five opponents. Serena topped the list.

When she played Serena, McHale wrote, her first thought was that, "I really hope I don't get killed. There's probably a better mentality to deploy for a match against the greatest female tennis player of all time, but that's what I was thinking." She went on to say, "She was my idol. She is my idol ... I felt like I was facing an icon. Everything you've heard about her unrivaled talent is accurate. If there were ever a perfectly constructed tennis player, Serena Williams is that player. She's powerful but precise. Intense but smooth. Competing against someone who has no weaknesses is overwhelming. You don't truly appreciate her greatness until you've played against her ... For Serena, being clutch is like breathing—it just happens instinctively."

rest of the year. The start of 2011 yielded even worse news, as Serena suffered several serious health scares, including a blood clot in one of her lungs, that kept her away from tennis for several months. People wondered if Serena would retire, but she managed to return for the US Open and almost won, losing in the finals.

A London Triple Play

In the summer of 2012, Serena once again returned to greatness in a place where she had shined in the past, London and Wimbledon. First, she won her fifth Wimbledon singles title, her first major championship in two years. Then, at the 2012 Summer Olympic Games, which were also held in London, Serena defeated Maria Sharapova at Wimbledon to claim her first Olympic gold medal in women's singles. The next day, she joined her sister Venus to win gold in women's doubles. Due to their dominance in both singles and doubles, Serena and Venus became the only two women to hold four tennis Olympic gold medals.

Serena continued her streak later that summer in New York City when she won the singles title at the US Open for the fourth time. Serena now owned fifteen Grand Slam singles titles and thirteen Grand Slam doubles titles. She ended the season going undefeated through the WTA Championships, winning the event for her third title. She capped 2012 by being named WTA Player of the Year for the fourth time as well as the International Tennis Federation World Champion.

After losing in the first round at the French Open the previous year, Serena returned in 2013 to claim her second title at Roland Garros, dethroning defending champion Sharapova. After Serena lost only one game in the semifinal, seven-time French Open champion Chris Evert described Serena's match as the finest female performance on clay she had ever seen.

"I'm still a little bit upset about that loss last year," Williams told ESPN after her victory. "But it's all about … how you recover … I've always said a champion isn't about how much they win, but it's about how they recover from their downs, whether it's an injury or whether it's a loss."

Making History

With her 2013 French Open win, Serena became only the fourth woman in the open era to win each Grand Slam tournament title at least twice, joining Martina Navratilova, Chris Evert, and Steffi Graf.

Serena suffered an upset loss in the fourth round at Wimbledon that summer, ending her career-best thirty-four match winning streak, but she came back to win another US Open, beating Victoria Azarenka for the second year in a row. With her victory, Serena became the oldest US Open champion at the age of nearly thirty-two. She also increased her total career tennis winnings to more than $50 million.

After experiencing a mixture of wins and losses for much of 2014, Serena managed to improve her game enough to win nineteen of twenty matches over a period that ended with her third straight US Open singles title and her sixth overall. Serena did not lose even one set in any match during the tournament. Serena finished the year strong, ranked number one in the world for the fourth time in her career. She held the top ranking for the entire calendar year, a feat not accomplished since Steffi Graf in 1996. She was also voted

Serena Williams shows off her 2014 US Open trophy, flanked by past champions Martina Navratilova (*left*) and Chris Evert (*right*).

Self-Reflection and Rebirth

WTA "Player of the Year" and ITF World Champion for the third consecutive year and her sixth time overall.

Serena continued to dominate as the next year began, beating Sharapova (again) for the 2015 Australian Open championship. The title was Serena's sixth Grand Slam singles title since she turned thirty; no one else has won more than three after that age. She also became the only player to win all four majors at least once after having turned thirty.

The following June, Serena managed to overcome an illness to win Roland Garros for the third time. During her childhood, Serena had begun to teach herself French, hoping someday to win the French Open and deliver her victory speech in that nation's language. She once again delighted the crowd when she addressed them in French, saying, "When I was a little girl, in California, my father and my mother wanted me to play tennis. And now I'm here, with twenty Grand Slam titles."

Another Serena Slam

Moving on to London that summer, the nearly thirty-four-year-old Serena overcame big sister Venus in the fourth round on her way to winning Wimbledon, becoming the oldest Grand Slam singles champion in the open era. Serena had now won four consecutive majors, thereby garnering her second career "Serena Slam."

Even more important at the time, Serena had won the first three of the four Grand Slam tournaments in 2015. The US Open beckoned, offering Serena another opportunity to accomplish what only three women had done before—win all four majors in a row in the same year, the coveted "calendar" Grand Slam.

Showing off her glamorous side, Serena Williams poses in her ballroom gown while attending the Wimbledon Winners Ball in July 2016.

Self-Reflection and Rebirth

Serena managed to defeat her sister Venus, this time in the quarterfinals. Her win left Serena just two victories away from her goal. But then, in an upset that shocked everyone in tennis, unseeded Italian player Roberta Vinci, ranked number forty-three in the world, overcame Serena in the semifinals even after badly losing the first set. Once again, the calendar slam would have to wait.

Despite her disappointment, Serena still excelled in 2015. She ranked number one for the whole season for the second consecutive year. She was also voted WTA "Player of the Year" for the seventh time. Then, in December, *Sports Illustrated* announced Williams as its "Sportsperson of the Year."

Serena Keeps Rolling

Serena Williams turned thirty-five on September 26, 2016. Yet, at an age when most professional athletes are well past their prime, Serena continued to play at the top levels of tennis.

On July 9, 2016, Serena won her seventh Wimbledon title. With twenty-two major titles, Serena tied Steffi Graf for the most major championships in the open era of professional tennis, which started when professional players were allowed to play along with amateurs in the major championships in 1968. Margaret Court won twenty-four majors, but most came when entry was restricted to amateurs. Then, just hours after her singles win, Serena and her sister Venus won the doubles championship for the sixth time.

Late that summer, Serena's quest for another US Open title ended in the semifinals, when she lost to up-and-coming Karolina Pliskova. Serena's loss caused her to fall from the number one ranking for the first time after 186 consecutive weeks, leaving her tied with Steffi Graf for the longest streak at number one in WTA history.

In January 2017 Serena regained her number one ranking when she defeated her sister Venus to claim her seventh Australian Open grand slam title. Serena's twenty-third Grand Slam singles title also placed her above Graf for the most women's Slam titles in the open era.

Serena's long and spectacular run of success has paid off. In 2016, *Forbes* magazine named Serena Williams the world's highest-paid female athlete for the previous twelve months. She earned nearly $9 million in tennis purses and an additional $20 million in endorsement fees. For her career, her $82 million in prize money more than doubles the total of the next highest player.

Williams now endorses many brands including Nike, Wilson, Beats, Delta Air Lines, and IBM. Serena also owns small portions of companies like Home Shopping Network and even a very small stake in the NFL's Miami Dolphins.

When asked in 2016 what she thought of Serena Williams's long tenure of success, eighteen-time Grand Slam Champion and current ESPN tennis commentator Chris Evert said that she is "the greatest tennis player that we've ever seen." Following Serena's Wimbledon championship victory over Angelique Kerber, Evert compared her career accomplishments to those of former champions like Steffi Graf, Martina Navratilova, and Billie Jean King, noting: "Now, I'd have to say that she's had the greatest results also."

Asked if she considers herself one of the greatest female athletes of all time, Williams responded: "I prefer the word 'one of the greatest athletes of all time.'"

Chapter 5

A Legacy Still in the Making

"I would like to leave a mark," Williams once said about her standing in the tennis world. "I think obviously I will, due to the fact that I'm doing something different in tennis."

There is no doubt that Serena Williams has already left an indelible mark in tennis. Yet, at the time of this writing, she is not even close to finishing her story. Her coach, Patrick Mouratoglou, recently told CNN that his target for Williams is thirty Slam titles. "Why not set up a record that will never be beaten in history? I think she can do it," he said.

But Serena's influence extends much further than tennis.

Building Her Brand

Serena became a media darling at a young age, and she has taken advantage of her talent and her fame to link her image with many different companies. Serena signed one of her first endorsement mega-deals with Puma in 1998, when she was only sixteen.

Opposite: Serena Williams and coach Patrick Mouratoglou share a laugh during a practice session. Mouratoglou believes that Serena can still win many more major championships.

Arnon Milchan, who owned Puma at the time and was also a Hollywood producer, said of Serena, "I thought when I bought Puma I could combine inner city, a Cinderella story, an African American girl going straight through the heart of the white man land and kick their butts."

Even then, Serena exuded confidence. When sixteen-year-old Serena visited him at his Hollywood Studio, Milchan described their meeting: "Serena [says] 'Excuse me sir. Do you have any doubt I will be number one in the world? ... What will you give me if I win the US Open this year?'" Milchan recalled that Serena asked for $1 million, then quickly doubled the amount. "So I said 'Ok, I will give you $2 million.' She said, 'Write it down.'" It took Serena only about a year to win the US Open.

Fashion has always been, and continues to be, one of Serena's greatest passions. Both she and Venus studied fashion design at the Art Institute of Fort Lauderdale, Florida, and each has extended her look on the court to establish separate businesses related to fashion, cosmetics, and jewelry.

In 2004, Serena started her own fashion line called Aneres (Serena spelled backward) and later partnered with fashion and shopping giant HSN. Models have displayed Serena's clothing on the covers of fashion magazines like *Elle*, *Glamour*, and *Vogue*. She also uses her clothing line to raise money for charity, including cancer research and the OWL Foundation (which was founded by her mother to help children with learning problems).

After buying her own apartment in Los Angeles, Serena expanded her interests to include acting. She has appeared in a number of television series including *ER*, *Law & Order: Special Victims Unit*, *My Wife and Kids*, and *Showtime's Street Time*, sometimes playing herself; she has also provided the voices for animated characters. In 2005, Serena and Venus appeared in their own television reality series, *Venus and Serena: For Real*. It ran for five episodes on the ABC Family network. They wanted to portray women working (at tennis and design), being successful, and living happy, fulfilled lives. They saw themselves as role models and wanted to show young people how to be successful, fulfilled, and happy, all at the same time.

Serena and Venus have written two books. *How to Play Tennis* teaches young tennis players about the game. *Venus and Serena: Serving from the Hip* talks about how to be successful and live a well-rounded life. Serena also wrote about her own life in her autobiography *Serena Williams: On The Line*, which was published in 2009.

Helping Others

Serena's influence extends well beyond tennis, money, or even creating fashion trends. She has made a conscious effort to make a difference in other people's lives, both in the United States and in other countries.

In her 2000 WTA Tour media guide entry, Serena, the defending US Open Champion, listed her most memorable achievement as "receiving an 'A' in geometry." Serena continues to focus on the importance of education for young people, especially those less fortunate.

Serena and Venus started a tennis academy in Los Angeles. In addition to playing tennis, the students participated in other activities, like going to museums and the movies. Serena used her foundation to open a school that bears her name in Kenya, Africa,

Serena Williams talks with students after opening the Serena Williams Secondary School outside of Nairobi, Kenya in 2008.

Serena Williams: Setting New Standards

in 2008. The Serena Williams Foundation also provides university scholarships for underprivileged students in the United States.

Over the years Serena has worked to support many other causes, including breast cancer, at-risk youth, earthquake victims in Haiti, and the UNICEF Schools for Asia campaign. She and Venus have played exhibition matches in different cities and donated the proceeds to Ronald McDonald House and other charities. In 2014, Serena began hosting an annual event described as "The Serena Williams Ultimate Fun Run," which helps underprivileged individuals and communities get equal access to education.

No matter what Serena does in her life, she is first and foremost a star tennis player, perhaps the best ever. While there are still more chapters to be written in Serena's tennis story, it's not too soon to speculate how she will be remembered.

A Fierce Competitor

Serena's long list of tennis titles and awards speaks for itself, but that is only part of the Serena Williams aura. Simply put, Serena Williams will be remembered as one of the most fierce and dynamic players ever. She has played fifteen different women in a Grand Slam final. Only five ever beat her, and only one (her sister Venus) managed to do that more than once.

When Serena Williams plays for the title, under pressure and against the best competition, she dominates. As of February 2017, her record in Grand Slam finals is 22-4 (84.6 percent), and in semifinals it is 26-4 (86.6 percent), a combined record of 48 and 8! Since she first became the number-one ranked player, nine other women have held that position. Serena has played those women 116 times in her career, winning an astounding 94 matches while losing only 22. This equates to winning 81 percent of all matches against other women who have risen to the number-one rank in the world.

Some players may resent Serena for her perceived lack of interaction with others on the tour, or maybe because she is just so good. But, it is also clear that Serena's success spurred other players to improve their game. Justine Henin-Hardenne of Belgium says that the Williams sisters motivated her to become stronger and fitter. Much smaller than either Serena or Venus, Henin-Hardenne hired a personal trainer to help increase the power of her serves and ground strokes. Amélie Mauresmo of France added weight training and cardiovascular workouts to her regimen to compete more effectively with the Williams sisters. Many other players did the same, and tennis also began to attract better female athletes into the sport.

A New Look

Serena and Venus certainly changed the look of tennis. Not only were they African American, but they played with beads in their hair and wore striking, very untraditional outfits.

Angela Haynes, a tennis pro, once said that, "As a tennis player myself, I'm thinking 'I wonder what Serena is going to wear at this Grand Slam.' ... Even people who don't care about tennis want to see what Serena is wearing."

In their book *Charging the Net: A History of Blacks in Tennis from Althea Gibson and Arthur Ashe to the Williams Sisters,* authors Cecil Harris and Larryette Kyle-DeBose talked about how Serena and Venus Williams changed the image of tennis:

Serena and Venus Williams changed the image of women's sports and challenged stereotypes of feminine beauty. The sisters prove that strong women can be beautiful as well as athletic.

A Legacy Still in the Making

The Williams sisters made tennis cool because they were so different—bolder, more aggressive, more athletic, more style-conscious than their tennis peers. Venus is the introvert with an almost regal sense of style … She is the angular, long-limbed power hitter … Serena is the curvaceous, sometimes tempestuous extrovert with the better all around game … Serena is the one who pushes the fashion envelope off the table.

African American tennis player James Blake rose from his roots in Harlem, New York, to be ranked in the Top Ten in 2006. Blake wrote the foreword for *Charging the Net* and talked about how important the Williams sisters had been for the sport, especially among African Americans who before who had little exposure to, or interest in, tennis:

I saw what happened with the Williams sisters when they were dominating tennis. I saw how many kids, especially African American girls, wanted to be like Venus and Serena. When I was first starting out on tour, every time I'd go through a security check-in or something similar, someone would ask me, "Do you know Venus and Serena?" … I hope I can have that kind of success and that kind of effect … It makes me proud to be part of the legacy of black players in tennis, along with Althea and Arthur, Venus and Serena, … and so many others.

Serena and Venus Williams expanded tennis past its country club roots and widened its appeal to the masses, particularly people of color. David Dinkins, former mayor of New York City, said in

2001 that "[Serena and Venus] have done for tennis ... what Tiger Woods did for golf. People who before had no interest in the sport, now have it."

The Race Factor

The sensitive subject of race cannot be dismissed when talking about Serena's career. Back in 1998, when Serena and Venus were just starting out, sportswriter Sally Jenkins wrote an article about how racism affected them on the tour. "The truth is that there is racism in tennis, and it had been directed at the Williamses, although it has rarely been explicit," Jenkins said. "Rather, it has been conveyed by innuendo and insinuation."

"The game [tennis] itself is not really an inviting place for people of color," said Kim Sands, a former women's head coach at the University of Miami. She went on to say that other sports like basketball and football have enough African American players where "there are enough people who look like you and are successful." She said, "There just aren't enough people of color who are successful in tennis ... Players can be from Sweden, Russia, Belgium, wherever, but they're all white, and they all gravitate to one another. They don't feel like they're alone."

Both Serena and Venus had been raised to be proud of who they were. "I wanted them to be women of color and proud ... and not let anyone make them ashamed of it, " their mother, Oracene Price, has said. "And that was the main purpose of the beads because it shows their heritage and where they come from."

Oracene also wanted her daughters to be something more than just successful African Americans. "Yes, they're black, that's pretty obvious," she said. "But they realize the person inside matters more

A Career of Accomplishment

Serena Williams is more than one of the best women's tennis players in history. Serena stands out as one of the most dominant and influential athletes and personalities of all time, male or female.

In January 2017, Serena passed Steffi Graf for the most Grand Slam singles titles (twenty-three) in the open era, leaving her just one win behind all-time leader Margaret Smith Court. Serena has won each Grand Slam singles title at least three times, including Wimbledon (seven), the US Open (six), the Australian Open (seven) and the French Open (three), as well as an Olympic singles gold medal. Along with her sister Venus, Serena also has won fourteen Slam doubles championships and three Olympic gold medals. Serena has also won two Grand Slams in mixed doubles.

Just as impressively, Serena's career has withstood the test of time. She won her first Grand Slam singles and doubles championships in 1999, when she was only seventeen. She won her latest in both categories in January 2017, at the age of thirty-five.

Serena Williams has won so many awards over the years that it would be difficult to list them all. She is a four-time winner of the Associated Press Female Athlete of the Year and has been named *Sports Illustrated's* "Best Female Athlete of the Decade." She's been honored by organizations such as Teen Choice, *Forbes*, ESPN, BET, Harris Interactive, and *Glamour* magazine. *Time* magazine named her to its one hundred Most Influential People list twice, in 2010 and 2014.

than the color of their skin. I think they want to be role models ...
for all kids, not just black kids."

Serena has always been conscious of her responsibility to
promote tennis to the African American community but also
to speak out when she saw situations that were unjust. In 2000,
Serena was scheduled to play in a tournament in South Carolina.
She withdrew, however, when she decided to support a boycott of
events in South Carolina organized by the National Association for
the Advancement of Colored People (NAACP) to protest South
Carolina's practice of flying the Confederate flag over its statehouse.

Confident Self Image

Despite her success in tennis and in life, Serena has found it difficult
to escape criticism about how she looks. For some people, Serena's
strong, muscular physique does not fit the traditional, "feminine"
image of the thin, graceful female athlete. Many of the negative
comments suggest sexist or racial stereotypes.

Serena has always been proud of her appearance, both on and
off the court. In an interview with *Good Morning America* in 2015,
she said: "I've been like this my whole life, and I embrace me and I
love how I look. I love that I am a full woman, and I'm strong and
I'm powerful and I'm beautiful at the same time." People obviously
agree, as Serena has been featured on countless magazine covers and
photo spreads, including *Glamour, Self, Fitness, Cosmopolitan,* and
Sports Illustrated.

Serena's attitude has helped other young women grow more
confident with their own self-image. She also encourages everyone
to look beyond appearances to find beauty. "My definition of beauty
is definitely a definition of how a person is inside," she has said.

"It doesn't matter how you look outside … you can be the most beautiful person on the outside but if you have a bad heart then it just makes a person to me unattractive."

Drama: The Sister Slams

When all is said and done, perhaps the most lasting image of Serena's career will show her standing on the court, steely-eyed, decked out in another amazing outfit, preparing to face her equally impressive sister Venus for the ultimate tennis prize: a Grand Slam singles title.

No movie could ever duplicate their real-life story: two of the best players ever, close in ability and age, competing against each other for two decades, yet remaining loving sisters and best friends throughout.

Cliff Drysdale, a former Hall of Fame player and commentator for ESPN, has said, "It's hard to compete against your best friend in a big match, or somebody from your own country. I can't imagine what it's like to compete against your own sister."

The Williams sisters have managed to handle it. After losing to Serena in five straight Grand Slam finals, Venus said, "People seemed to think I was going to be devastated. I guess they assumed that jealousy would eat away at me and that our relationship would change for the worse … Whatever happens on the tennis court, it's not going to change my love for Serena or my pride in her accomplishments."

Serena also said, "Long before fans and reporters knew us, our parents taught us that our relationship is much more important than being successful in tennis or getting ahead in the world."

Proving the truth of their statements, people were stunned that, after Serena beat Venus at the French Open final in 2002,

Venus retrieved her own camera and joined other photographers to snap pictures of Serena holding the champions' cup. Their ability to compete yet remain close serves as a testament to their own character, the way they were raised, and also how their personalities in many ways complement rather than contradict each other.

No discussion of the dynamic Serena-Venus rivalry would be complete without considering a final, intriguing question: How many more tournaments could they have won if they did not have to compete against each other?

Serena and Venus have played twenty-eight times, including fifteen Grand Slams. Serena leads her sister 17-11 overall and 7-2 in Grand Slam finals. If Venus did not eliminate her sister in those eleven matches, would Serena have won even more titles than she has to date?

Venus discovered in 2011 at the age of thirty-one that she suffers from a medical condition known as Sjogren's syndrome, an autoimmune disease that causes severe joint pain, swelling, numbness, and fatigue. Despite her condition, Venus continues to play, and the Serena-Venus story has yet to write its final chapter.

Influence Beyond Tennis

In 2010, *Time* magazine named Serena Williams to its list of the one hundred most influential people in the world, not just for her tennis accomplishments, but also for her work in promoting education in the United States and Africa.

For each person it selected, *Time* asked one of their peers to help explain why they were chosen. Billie Jean King, a former tennis champion well known for her work promoting women's rights, wrote this about Serena:

Serena Williams continues to win tennis championships, collect awards, and chase her dreams.

Serena Williams: Setting New Standards

Serena Williams is one of those rare champions who have transcended sports and impacted our society. In tennis, she is as focused … as she has ever been [but she is also] committed to making a difference in the lives of others. Her work with children in Kenya and here in the US stresses the importance of education. Through her charitable efforts, people are seeing her in a larger context.

Serena once said, "One of the most important things you can do for yourself is envision a fantastic future. Dreams give you a direction in life. Everyone who is successful started with one."

Serena Williams has certainly chased her dreams, forever changing the perception of not only what it means to be a tennis star, but an African American woman as well.

Timeline

September 26, 1981 Serena Jameka Williams is born in Saginaw, Michigan.

October 28, 1995 Serena Williams plays her first professional match.

September 11, 1999 Serena wins her first Grand Slam singles title at the US Open, defeating Martina Hingis.

March 17, 2001 Serena is booed while winning the title at Indian Wells and vows she will never return.

September 8, 2001 Serena and Venus play each other for the first time in a major at the US Open. Venus wins.

June 8, 2002 Serena defeats Venus to win her first French Open title, proving she could win on slow clay surfaces.

January 25, 2003 Serena wins the Australian Open for the first time and completes the "Serena Slam."

September 14, 2003 Older sister Yetunde Price is shot and killed in Los Angeles by a gang member.

January 27, 2007 Serena wins the Australian Open for the third time, defeating Maria Sharapova.

July 7, 2010 Serena steps on glass at a restaurant in Munich, Germany, cutting a tendon and requiring surgery.

Serena Williams can't hide her emotions upon returning to Indian Wells in 2015 to play in that event for the first time in fourteen years.

Feb. 19, 2011 Serena is hospitalized in Los Angeles after developing a pulmonary embolism. Later that month, she requires emergency treatment for a hematoma in her stomach.

Aug. 4, 2012 Serena Williams completes the "Golden Slam" (singles titles in all four Grand Slams as well as the Olympic singles gold medal) by winning the women's singles gold medal at the London Olympics.

September 7, 2014 Serena wins the US Open singles title, her eighteenth Grand Slam. She tied Chris Evert and Martina Navratilova in career major titles won.

March 13, 2015 Serena returns to play Indian Wells for the first time in fourteen years.

July 11, 2015 Serena completes another "Serena Slam" by winning Wimbledon.

July 9, 2016 Serena wins Wimbledon, adding a twenty-second Grand Slam singles title to tie Steffi Graf in the open era.

December 29, 2016 Serena announces her engagement to Alexis Ohanian, the cofounder of Reddit.

January 19, 2017 Serena beats Venus in the Australian Open final, adding a twenty-third Grand Slam singles title to her remarkable career. She also extended her own record for oldest woman to win a Grand Slam singles title to age thirty-five.

Glossary

academies Schools or places of instruction.

brackets The groups that tennis players are placed in to determine the schedule of matches.

doubles Tennis between two teams of two players each. Mixed doubles features teams of one woman and one man.

draw The schedule of matches in a tennis tournament, including all brackets.

endorsements Helping to sell products by appearing in ads and publicly supporting the product in return for payment from the company that makes the product.

fault A tennis serve that does not land in the service box. A second serve is granted if the fault occurs during first serve; the point is lost if it occurs during a second serve (double fault).

ghetto A rundown area of a city in which many people live.

Grand Slam The four major tennis championships: the Australian Open, the French Open, Wimbledon (England), and the US Open. Also refers to winning the four tournaments in a row.

hindsight The ability to understand an event or situation only after it has happened.

icon A person who is considered a representative symbol of something excellent.

Jehovah's Witnesses A form of Christianity that believes salvation is obtained by a combination of faith, good works, and obedience but does not believe that Jesus is divine.

juniors Tennis tournaments for players under the age of eighteen.

legacy A person's long-term influence and contributions that last over time.

match point Where a player is one point away from winning the match.

open era The open era began in 1968 when the Grand Slam tournaments agreed to allow professional players to compete with amateurs. Before 1968, only amateurs were allowed to compete in the Grand Slam tournaments.

probation A period of time when a person must observe good behavior and follow the rules to avoid incurring a penalty.

professional An athlete who plays in tournaments for money.

seeded The position at which a player is ranked against others during a tournament, usually restricted to the top sixteen or thirty-two players in a draw.

segregated People are separated or divided by sex, race or religion.

serve The first shot a player hits from behind the baseline to start a point.

sets Groups of tennis games. The first player to win six games with a two-game advantage wins the set. Women must win two sets to win a match. In some tournaments, including Grand Slams, men must win three sets to win a match.

singles A match where single players compete against each other.

tiebreaker A game played in a match when a set reaches six games won for each side. The first player or team to win seven points (and is at least two points ahead) wins the tiebreaker and the set.

tournaments Events in which several rounds of competition are played to determine the winner.

WTA Women's Tennis Association; the governing body of professional women's tennis.

Further Information

Books

Aronson, Virginia. *Venus and Serena Williams: Women Who Win.* Philadelphia: Chelsea House Publishers, 2001.

Bailey, Diane. *Venus and Serena Williams: Tennis Champions.* New York: The Rosen Publishing Group, Inc., 2010.

Uschan, Michael V. *Serena Williams.* Farmington Hills, MI: Lucent Books, 2011.

Williams, Serena. *On The Line.* New York: Grand Central Publishing, 2009.

Williams, Serena, and Venus Williams. *How to Play Tennis.* New York: DK Publishing, 2004.

Websites

Serena Williams's Facebook Page

https://www.facebook.com/SerenaWilliams
Fans can keep up with Serena Williams through her social media posts.

Serena Williams website

http://www.serenawilliams.com
The official website of the tennis champion includes links to photos of the player, her blog, news stories, her tournament results, her sponsors, and ways to buy products she endorses.

United States Tennis Association

https://www.usta.com
The official website of the USTA provides tips, news stories, tournament schedules, and more for amateur and pro players.

The US Open

http://www.usopen.org/index.html
The official website of the US national championship provides news, videos, scores, and social media links for fans of tennis.

Women's Tennis Association

http://www.wtatennis.com/
The governing body for women's professional tennis provides information on the tour and the players who compete on it.

Videos

Serena at Wimbledon: Still I Rise

http://www.wtatennis.com/news/article/5716648
Before winning Wimbledon in 2015, Serena Williams recited the poem "Still I Rise" by late poet and author Maya Angelou in a video montage complied by the BBC. The video shows scenes from Serena's career as the audio plays in the background.

Serena Williams and Venus Williams as Children— Rare videos and Interview!

https://www.youtube.com/watch?v=DvQEXJW6ZR4
Videos and interviews of Serena and Venus when they were young.

Serena Williams—Mini Biography

http://www.biography.com/people/serena-williams-9532901/
videos/serena-williams-mini-biography-2192498386
A mini-biography of Serena Williams that runs about three minutes
long from Biography.com.

Serena Williams Tennis Outfits 2000-2013

https://www.youtube.com/watch?v=1c3X-pu2sbg
A montage of Serena Williams' fashions that she has worn while on
the tennis court.

2016, Day 12 Highlights, Serena Williams vs. Angelique Kerber

https://www.youtube.com/watch?v=7mp9ou50gEA
Highlights of Serena Williams playing Angelique Kerber in the 2016
Wimbledon final.

Bibliography

Books

Bryant, Jill. *Women Athletes Who Changed the World.* New York: The Rosen Publishing Group, Inc., 2012.

Donaldson, Madeline. *Venus & Serena Williams.* Minneapolis: Lerner Publications Company, 2011.

Harris, Cecil, and Larryette Kyle-DeBose. *Charging the Net: A History of Blacks in Tennis from Althea Gibson and Arthur Ashe to the Williams Sisters.* Chicago: Ivan R. Dee, 2007.

Stewart, Mark. *Venus & Serena Williams: Sisters in Arms.* Brookfield, CT: The Millbrook Press, 2000.

Todd, Anne M. *Venus and Serena Williams: Athletes.* New York: Chelsea House Publishers, 2009.

Wertheim, L. Jon. *Venus Envy: A Sensational Season Inside the Women's Tennis Tour.* New York: HarperCollins Publishers, Inc., 2001.

Williams, Richard. *Black and White: The Way I See It.* New York: Atria Books, 2014.

Websites

"ATA History: History of the American Tennis Association." AmericanTennisAssociation.org. Accessed October 12, 2016. http://www.americantennisassociation.org/ata-history/

Badenhausen, Kurt. "Celebrating 35 Years of Serena Williams (By The Numbers)" Forbes.com. September 26, 2016. http://www. forbes.com/sites/kurtbadenhausen/2016/09/26/celebrating-35-years-of-serena-williams-by-the-numbers/#28fe30161511

Biography.com editors. "Serena Williams Biography." Biography. com. September 12, 2016. http://www.biography.com/people/ serena-williams-9532901

Caple, Jim. "New Heights For Serena Williams."" ESPN.com. June 7, 2013. http://www.espn.com/espnw/news-commentary/ article/9352085/2013-french-open-serena-williams-looks-better-ever-heading-final-maria-sharapova

Glass, Alana. "This Week In Women's Sports: Serena Williams Wins 22nd Grand Slam, Hope Solo Records Career Shutouts." Forbes.com. July 10, 2016. http://www.forbes.com/sites/ alanaglass/2016/07/10/this-week-in-womens-sports-serena-williams-wins-22nd-grand-slam-hope-solo-records-career-shutouts/#4ef7ce855013

Hodgkinson, Mark. "Martina Hingis Praises Williams Sisters Ahead Of Wimbledon Showdown." espnW.com. July 5, 2015. http://www. espn.com/espnw/news-commentary/article/13201912/martina-hingis-praises-williams-sisters-ahead-wimbledon-showdown

McGrogan, Ed. "Serena Routs Zvonareva For Fourth Wimbledon title." Tennis.com. July 3, 2010. http://www.tennis.com/pro-game/2010/07/serena-routs-zvonareva-for-fourth-wimbledon-title/23255

McHale, Christina. "The Five Toughest Players I've Ever Faced." ThePlayersTribune.com. July 28, 2016. http://www.theplayerstribune.com/christina-mchale-tennis-five-toughest-opponents/

Roberts, Selena. "Tennis; Serena Williams Wins As the Boos Pour Down." NYTimes.com. March 18, 2001. http://www.nytimes.com/2001/03/18/sports/tennis-serena-williams-wins-as-the-boos-pour-down.html

"Serena Williams: All The Accomplishments From A Remarkable Career." USAToday.com. August 9, 2016. http://www.usatoday.com/story/sports/olympics/rio-2016/2016/08/09/serena-williams-olympics-grand-slam/88442570/

"20 Key Moments For The One And Only Serena Williams. " ESPN.com. May 20, 2015. http://www.espn.com/espnw/news-commentary/article/12908223/20-key-moments-one-only-serena-williams

"The World"s Highest Paid Athletes." Forbes.com. Accessed October 17, 2016. http://www.forbes.com/profile/serena-williams/

Ziller, Tom. "15 Reasons Serena Williams Is The Greatest." SBNation.com. December 15, 2015. http://www.sbnation.com/2015/8/31/9193409/15-reasons-serena-williams-us-open-greatest

DVDs

Raising Tennis Aces: The Williams Story. Santa Monica, CA. Terry Jervis, 2002.

Venus And Serena. Los Angeles, CA: Maiken Baird and Michelle Major, 2012.

Index

Page numbers in **boldface** are illustrations. Entries in **boldface** are glossary terms.

About the Author

Gerry Boehme is an author, editor, speaker and business consultant who loves to travel and to learn about new things. Gerry has written books for students dealing with many subjects, including famous people who have made a difference in other people's lives. He has also written for magazines and has spoken at conferences around the world. Gerry graduated from The Newhouse School at Syracuse University and lives on Long Island, New York, with his wife and two children.